HUSH LITTLE BABY

A FOLK LULLABY

ILLUSTRATED BY ALIKI

PRENTICE-HALL, INC. ENGLEWOOD CLIFFS, N. J.

Hush Little Baby

Illustrated by Aliki Brandenberg.

All rights reserved.

Library of Congress Catalog Card Number:

68-12194

ISBN: 0-13-448167-4
ISBN: 0-13-448175-5 pbk.

10 **9**

FOR

JASON

Hush, little baby, don't say a word,

Papa's gonna buy you a mockingbird.

If that mockingbird don't sing,

Papa's gonna buy you a diamond ring.

If that diamond ring turns brass,

Papa's gonna buy you a looking glass.

If that looking glass gets broke,

Papa's gonna buy you a billy goat.

If that billy goat won't pull,

Papa's gonna buy you a cart and bull.

If that cart and bull turn over,

Papa's gonna buy you a dog named Rover.

If that dog named Rover won't bark,

Papa's gonna buy you a horse and cart.

If that horse and cart fall down,

You'll still be the sweetest little

baby in town.

Hush, little baby, don't say a word
Papa's gonna buy you a mockingbird.

If that mockingbird don't sing
Papa's gonna buy you a diamond ring.

If that diamond ring turns brass,
Papa's gonna buy you a looking glass.

If that looking glass gets broke,
Papa's gonna buy you a billy goat.

If that billy goat won't pull,
Papa's gonna buy you a cart and bull.

If that cart and bull turn over,
Papa's gonna buy you a dog named Rover.

If that dog named Rover don't bark,
Papa's gonna buy you a horse and cart.

If that horse and cart fall down,
You'll still be the sweetest little baby in town.

HUSH LITTLE BABY

Hush, lit-tle ba- by   don't say a word,

Pa-pa's gon-na buy   you a mock-ing bird.

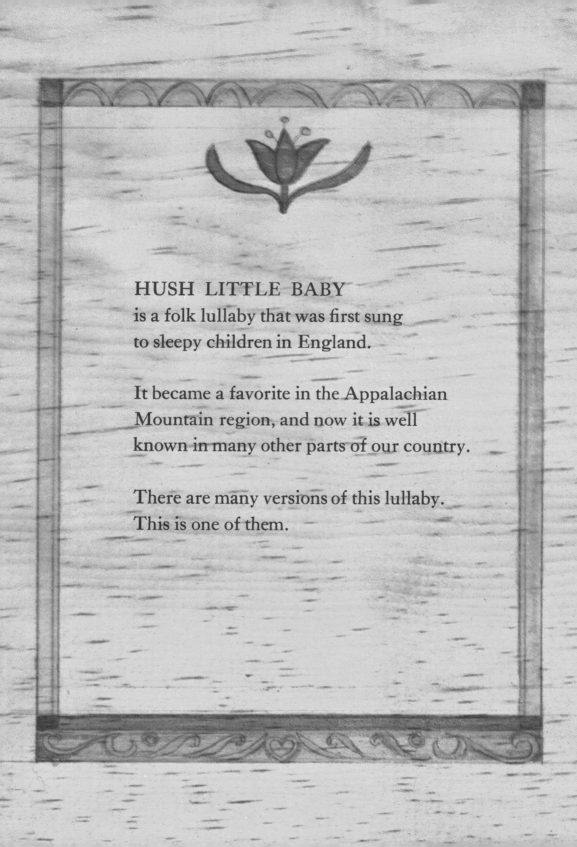

HUSH LITTLE BABY
is a folk lullaby that was first sung
to sleepy children in England.

It became a favorite in the Appalachian
Mountain region, and now it is well
known in many other parts of our country.

There are many versions of this lullaby.
This is one of them.